HELPFUL HINTS

COLOR: The wedding color scheme usually revolves around the attendants' gowns. It is important to choose flowers that compliment and enhance the color of the gown, accenting the look of the total wedding. Do not try to match flowers and ribbons exactly to the color of the gowns. They will fade into the background of the dress and will not even be noticed. Rather, blend the colors for a co-ordinated look.

CHOOSING FLOWERS: Take along a swatch of the dress fabric when purchasing flowers. Make a list of everyone who will need flowers and, if possible, make an appointment so you will get personalized help and attention.

RECEPTION FLOWERS: These are smaller bouquets in vases used to decorate tables at the reception. To transport these flowers to the reception without crushing the flowers or damaging the bows, insert the stems of the completed bouquets (with the bows attached) into a sheet of styrofoam®. Place them side by side. When you arrive at the reception, it is quick and easy to place the bouquets in vases and there is no need to arrange the flowers. See page 13 where Mother's Presentation Bouquet is made into a smaller size to be used at the reception.

CANDLES: A note of caution, never leave a burning candle unattended.

ACRYLIC SPRAY: Most of the designs in this book call for matte acrylic spray. The designers have found that giving the finished arrangement a coat of acrylic spray will add sizing to the fabric of the flowers and will help prevent dried flowers from breaking. One note, to prevent spotting, cover goblets, cake knives, crystal vases, candle holders, etc., with tissue paper before spraying the floral design.

FLORAL TAPE: It does not have a right or a wrong side nor does it stick like Scotch Tape™. It will become tacky and adhere to itself when stretched. See the illustration below and notice that the tape is held next to the stem with the left hand and stretched diagonally along the stem, overlapping as you go. Cut or tear the tape at the end and press the end to seal.

TO REINFORCE OR LENGTHEN FLOWER STEMS: Lay a piece of wire next to the end of the flower. Wrap with floral tape and gently pull so the tape will stick to itself. Floral tape all the way to the end of the stem or wire.

TO SEPARATE FLOWERS: Most silk and dried flowers come on a main stem. It is often necessary to cut the flowers from that stem. If the stems are short or limp, follow the directions above to reinforce or lengthen flower stems with wire and floral tape.

PIERCING: This is another method of wiring heads of flowers for corsages. It is sometimes necessary to remove the heads of flowers from the main stem and pierce the calyx (the green part under the flower blossom). Heat one end of a 22 or 26 gauge wire by holding it in a candle flame. Immediately pierce the calyx and insert half the length of wire. Bend both wire ends down to form a stem. Tape the wire pieces together.

A PERSONAL NOTE: When your wedding day arrives, enjoy this special time with your family and friends. The day will go by rapidly. If everything doesn't go exactly as planned, please try to keep calm and call on your sense of humor. Believe us, you'll be the only person to know. Make it a special day to remember!

Heart Bouquet

YOU WILL NEED:

3 1/2" wide styrofoam® bouquet holder
15 lt. pink roses, each 1 1/2" long & 1 1/4" wide
3 stems stephanotis (each stem has 5 clusters of flowers with leaves)
2 stems rose leaves (each stem has 7 sprigs of 3 leaves per sprig)
1 stem white silk baby's breath
1 stem purple heather with 10 clusters
2 stems dark pink blossoms, each 1/2" wide (each stem has 14 flowers and 5 buds)
5 yards of 1/8" wide orchid ribbon
5 yards 1/8" wide colonial rose ribbon
5 yards 3/8" wide white lace ribbon
18 pieces of 18 gauge wire, each 18" long
white cloth covered wire
green floral tape
white floral tape
matte acrylic spray

1

2

3

4

1   Cut apart the rose leaves from the main stem leaving 3 leaves per sprig. Use green floral tape to add a 3" length of wire to each sprig (see page 1). Insert 7 sprigs around the outer edge of the bouquet holder--to make the heart shape place the bottom center leaf 5 1/2" out from the foam and the two upper leaves 5" from the foam. The other leaves are 4" from the foam.

2   Cut the roses apart and re-stem if necessary (see page 1). Insert a rose at the top center of the bouquet so it is 2 1/2" from the foam. Place the bottom and top two roses 4" from the foam at about the same angle as the leaves.

3   Insert the remaining four roses so they are 3" from the foam but keep them at the same angle as the leaves.

4   Insert one rose in the center of the bouquet 4" from the foam. The other roses are placed at an angle halfway between the center rose and the outer roses, 3" from the foam. The bouquet should have a rounded look from the top rose to the outer edge.

5

6

5 Cut the stephanotis clusters of two to four flowers from the stem--keep the greens attached. Each cluster should be 4 1/2" to 5 1/2" from the bottom stem to the highest flower. If necessary, lengthen stems with 18 gauge wire and green floral tape (see page 1).

6 Insert the stephanotis clusters between the roses, keeping the greens close to the foam.

7

8

7 The remaining rose tri-leaf sprigs are inserted at an angle around the center roses, facing the center of the bouquet.

8 Cut the clusters of baby's breath, heather and blossoms. If necessary, add a 3 1/2" wire to each cluster (see page 1). Insert each type of flower evenly throughout the bouquet so the color is evenly distributed.

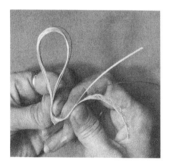

9

10

9 For each ribbon and lace tuft: cut a 9" length of each ribbon and the lace. Hold the three pieces together and handle as one. Begin at one end and make a 3" long loop. Then fold up the loose ends as shown.

10 Wrap the bottom 1/8" of ribbons and lace tightly with a 6" piece of cloth covered wire. Add a 3 1/2" length of wire and wrap with green floral tape. Cut the ribbon and lace ends at an angle. Make 7 tufts.

11 Insert one tuft in the center of the bouquet and evenly space the others throughout the bouquet.

11

12

12 For the streamers: place the ribbons and lace together and handle as one. Measure 32" from one end and make a loop. Make two more loops each longer than the last. Hold the loops together with a 6" piece of cloth covered wire. Attach the streamers to the front of the bouquet holder at the handle, twist the wire ends. Use white floral tape to cover the wire ends and the handle of the holder. Spray with matte acrylic spray.

Cake Top

YOU WILL NEED:

1 plastic cake top holder with lace trim
3" wide white styrofoam® ball
1/3 yard of 1 1/2" wide pink acetate
*   ribbon*
2 stems of ivy (each stem has 3 sprigs
*   of 1 1/2" to 2 1/2" long leaves)*
12 lt. pink roses, each 1 1/4" long
1 stem lt. pink alstromeria (the stem has
*   8 flowers and 4 buds), each flower*
*   is 2 1/2" wide*
15 sprigs of white lily of the valley
1 stem of purple silk heather (with 10
*   clusters)*
15 pieces of 18 gauge wire, each 18"
*   long*
green floral tape
Aleene's Original Tacky Glue
matte acrylic spray

1

1. Lift the lace skirt on the cake top. Run a bead of craft glue just below the top of the lace. Press the ribbon into the glue, gathering where necessary. Keep the bottom edge of the ribbon even with the bottom of the cake top.

2. Trim the bottom and sides of the styrofoam® ball to fit in the cake top. The top of the foam should be 1/2" to 3/4" above the edge of the cup. Glue the ball into the cup.

2

3

3. The roses should have the following stem lengths: one at 8", three at 7", four at 5 1/2", four at 5". Leave the greens on the stems if possible. If necessary, lengthen the rose stems with 18 gauge wire and green floral tape (see page 1).

4. Insert the 5" long roses evenly spaced around the base of the cup, parallel to the table. Each rose extends 3" from the edge of the foam.

4

5

6

5   Place the 8" long rose in the center of the styrofoam®. The top of the rose will be about 10" from the table.

6   Insert the four 5 1/2" long roses above and between the roses in the first layer. Angle these roses into the center of the ball and keep them 3 1/2" to 4" from the foam to the top of the flower.

7

8

7   Place the three 7" long roses in a triangle about 2" from the center rose. Insert these at an angle. All roses should be arranged in a stair-step fashion.

8   The alstromeria stems should be as follows: four with buds at 7" and four single flowers at 5 1/2". Insert the 5 1/2" long flowers between the bottom roses, alternating flowers with buds and single flowers. Position the other stems between the second and third layers of roses, angle all stems toward the center.

9

10

9   Cut apart the ivy sprigs, add wire to lengthen stems if necessary (see page 1). Make one 9" long, three at 7", six at 5" and four single leaves at 3" long. Insert the 9" sprig so it shows about 2" above the center rose. Place the 7" stems in a triangle between the second and third layers of roses.

10   Insert the four single ivy leaves at the base to cover the styrofoam®. Then drape some double ivy sprigs over the edge of the cup. Fill in with the rest of the ivy as needed.

11

12

11   Separate the heather clusters and add wire lengths of 5" to 7" long (see page 1). Insert the heather clusters evenly throughout the design.

12   Re-stem the lily of the valley sprigs at lengths of 6" to 9". Place throughout the arrangement making sure they extend slightly beyond the roses. Spray with matte acrylic spray.

Flowers for the Cake

6

FOR EACH YOU WILL NEED:

1 dk. red rose, 1 1/4" long
2 lily of the valley sprigs
1 ivy leaf section with 2 leaves
1 yd. 1/2" wide pink acetate ribbon
26 gauge wire
green floral tape
matte acrylic apray

Make as many as necessary to lay between the layers and around the bottom of the cake.

1

2

1   Tape a 2" piece of wire to each lily of the valley sprig and the ivy leaf section. Add wire to the rose if necessary, floral tape the stem.

2   For the bow: Follow the directions on page 21, steps 5-8, to make a bow with 6 loops (each 1 1/2" long) and 2 cover loops. Leave 2" long streamers.

3

4

3   Place the rose in the center of the ivy. Add a lily of the valley sprig to each side and floral tape together.

4   Add the bow and tape. Trim the ribbon ends to 1". Tape the exposed wires. Spray with matte acrylic spray.

Laurel

YOU WILL NEED:

1 stem of white roses, each 1" across
    (the stem has 6 roses and 3 buds)
1 stem of white silk baby's breath
1 stem of purple silk heather
7 dk. pink blossoms, each 1/2" wide
    plus 4 buds
10 pearl sprays
30 rose leaves, each 3/4" wide and
    1" long
8 pieces of 22 gauge wire, each 18"
    long
green floral tape
matte acrylic spray

1

2

1 Leaving a 2" stem, cut from the main
   stems the roses, rose buds, blossoms,
   blossom buds, clusters of baby's
   breath and 6 clusters of heather (each
   3/4" wide). If necessary, add a length
   of 22 gauge wire to make a 2" long
   stem (see page 1).

2 Wrap floral tape around 1 1/2 pieces of
   wire.

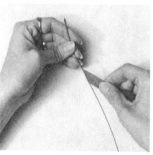

3

4

3 To make the construction easier:
   separate the different groups of
   flowers, leaves, baby's breath, and
   pearls.

4 Begin 1" from the end of the wire, lay a
   leaf stem and attach with floral tape to
   the wire. Leaves, pearls and baby's
   breath clusters are taped to the wire at
   the base of each item as shown.

5

6

5. When attaching any of the roses, blossoms and heather to the wire, begin wrapping the floral tape 1/2" below the bottom of the flower. Thus, 1/2" of the flower stem will show and will allow you to bend the flower as desired. Tape a rose to the wire.

6. Measure about 1/2" and tape a stem of baby's breath to the wire. Measure about 1/2" more and tape a dk. pink blossom to the wire.

7

8

7. Measure about 1/2" and tape another leaf to the wire. Measure 1/2" more and tape a pearl stem to the wire.

8. Measure about 1/2" and tape a cluster of heather to the wire. Measure 1/2" more and add another sprig of baby's breath. Repeat steps 4 through 8 to cover the wire, alternate buds and full flowers. Bend the items out from the main stem to keep an airy look.

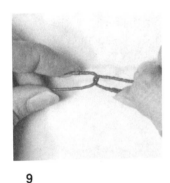

9

10

9. When the laurel is about 12" long, attach a 9" length of floral tape covered wire by making a 1" hook on each wire--adjust if necessary to fit the head. Hook the wires together and pinch. Floral tape over the ends.

10. Fill in with additional flowers, leaves or pearls to complete the piece. Give a coat of matte acrylic spray.

11

12

11. To add veiling: leave a 6" space at the back of the laurel. Gather the veiling with a needle and thread. Fold the gathered edge over the wire and whip stitch to the laurel.

12. To add ribbons: leave a 4" space at the back of the laurel. Make a bow with 18" long streamers and 2" long loops. Attach to the laurel with the wire from the bow. Floral tape over the wires. Flowers can be glued or tied to the streamers.

A Beautiful Basket

YOU WILL NEED:

basket--this one is 9" wide x 14" long x 4" high, the handle is 13" from table
3 yards of 3/8" wide orchid feather edge (picot) ribbon
4 yards of 1 3/4" wide gathered white lace
Spanish moss
1 stem each of pink, white and dk. pink roses, each rose is 1" wide (each stem has 6 roses and 3 buds)
21 rose tri-leaves, each 1/2" to 1 3/4" long
1 stem of lavender silk heather
1 stem of purple silk heather
glue gun
matte acrylic spray

This basket can hold cards from wedding guests, rice roses, the wedding programs or, when made smaller, it makes a lovely basket for the flower girl.

1   Glue the gathered lace to the inside and outside brim of the basket. Notice there is a 1" space between the edges of the lace. Wrap the feather edge ribbon around the handle of the basket about 12 times. Glue down the ends.

2   Glue lace to the under side of the handle on each side. Keep the lace edges close together. Glue a piece of feather edge ribbon to cover the lace edges. Make two bows, each 3" across and glue to the handle as shown above.

3   Glue Spanish moss around the top rim of the basket; keep it as compact as possible. Trim as necessary.

4   Cut the flowers and leaves from their stems leaving a 1/2" stem on each item. Glue each color rose to the rim, carefully dispersing the colors. Then glue each color of heather around the rim. Finally, fill in with the leaves. To give dimension, glue the items at slight angles. Spray generously with matte acrylic spray.

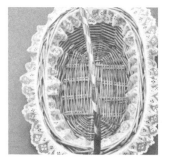

1

2

3

4

Rice Roses

FOR EACH ROSE YOU WILL NEED:

*1/4 yard of 3 3/4" wide white lace
    ribbon with scalloped edges
18" of 18 gauge wire
white cloth covered wire
green floral tape
1 rose leaf, 2" long
1/3 yard of 1/8" wide ribbon to match
    wedding colors
rice*

*Rice roses, rice bags or favors are a
lovely way to give your wedding
guests a personal memento of this
special day.*

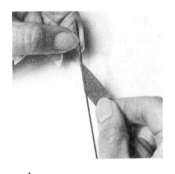

1   Floral tape a 6" length of 18 gauge wire.

2   Cut the lace ribbon in half lengthwise--each piece will be used to make one rose.

3   Place the lace right side down. Begin at one end of the lace and fold it over 1". Fold again.

4   Place the taped 18 gauge wire on the top center of the fold, 3/4" from the bottom edge. Fold this section of lace in half over the wire.

1

2

3

4

5

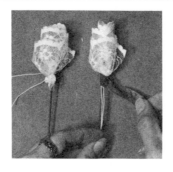

6

7

8

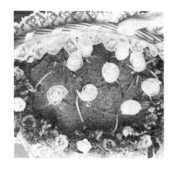

9

10

11

12

5 Hold the folded lace tightly around the wire. Wrap the lace around the wire, gathering the bottom edge of lace as you go. The scallops on the lace should descend slightly as you rotate the lace.

6 Wrap a 6" piece of cloth covered wire securely around the gathered bottom edge of lace. Floral tape over the gathers.

7 Place the leaf next to the rose and floral tape to the stem. Tie a bow with the 1/8" wide ribbon around the stem.

8 Fill the middle of the rose half full of rice or birdseed. Grasp the top inside edge of lace and rotate the stem several times to form a very tight bud at the center.

9 The roses are best kept upright in a basket. Wire a piece of green styrofoam® into a basket and insert the rose stems into the foam (the Beautiful Basket on page 9 looks great).

10 To release the rice or birdseed, hold the stem firmly and with a forward motion of the wrist, the contents will be released.

11 Rice bags are made using an 8" circle of fabric or fine netting. Fill with rice or birdseed and tie with 1/8" wide ribbon.

12 Favors are also made with an 8" circle of fabric or netting. Fill with colored mints and tie with a 1/8" wide ribbon. Tiny flowers or baby's breath are a nice touch at the bow.

Hair Clip

YOU WILL NEED:

1 hair clip
2 pink roses, each 1" wide plus a bud
3 clusters of purple silk heather
5 rose leaves, each 3/4" wide
3 pearl sprays (3 strands per spray)
1 yard of 1/16" wide white & silver
   ribbon
1 yard of 1/8" wide colonial rose ribbon
white cloth covered wire
glue gun

A hair comb can be made similar to this hair clip. Streamers may be eliminated and a bow with 1 1/2" long loops is used.

Optional: individual pearls may be glued to the streamers using tweezers to dip the pearls into Aleene's Original Tacky Glue and set on each side of the ribbons.

1. Place both ribbons together and handle as one. Measure 6" from one end and make 8 loops, each 1" long. Fold a 6" piece of cloth covered wire and slip in the center of the bow, twist the wire ends to secure the ribbons. Set aside.

2. To prevent gluing the hair clip shut, place a piece of cardboard in the clip. Cut the stems from the leaves and glue to the clip--3 on top of the clip handle and 2 toward the opening, slightly angle the leaves.

3. Cut the stems from the pearl sprays. Glue one spray to each side of the clip. Place them so the pearls extend 1" beyond the leaves. Glue the bow diagonally across the leaves.

4. Cut the roses and heather clusters from the main stem. Glue a rose on each side of the bow. The bud goes among the ribbon loops. The heather clusters are glued between the roses. Separate the pearl strands and glue each into the center of the bow.

1

2

3

4

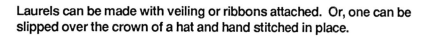

Laurels can be made with veiling or ribbons attached. Or, one can be slipped over the crown of a hat and hand stitched in place.

The Mother's Presentation Bouquet adds a colorful touch on the tables at a reception.

Rather than tucking the Three Rose Corsage away, wire it to the lid of a basket—use to hold cosmetics or jewelry.

Large Sprays in a peach and turquoise color combination for the bride and groom glasses. Smaller Sprays are elegant on the candles for a 25th Anniversary or dinner party.

An Over The Shoulder Corsage can be wired to a wicker mat for a wall decoration. Or, it can be attached to the handle of a basket for an attractive and practical addition to the bath. Or shape the corsage and wire to a lace wedding fan to be carried by the bride instead of a bouquet.

Peach, white and turquoise are the colors used in the Laurel surrounding the unity candle, for the flower girl basket, on the Cake Top, and in the Three Flower Corsage attached to the parasol. The corsage can be removed from the parasol and worn during the reception.

The Shoe Clip can be used as a table favor to hold place cards or (with the wires bent) as a napkin ring.

Dusty pink and burgundy are the colors in this Heart Bouquet.

Stephanotis and ivy form this Pew Decoration.

The Heart Bridal Train Holder can be suspended with fishing line above the table for a bridal shower decoration. After the wedding the Holder can be hung on the wall for decoration or incorporated into a wall grouping.

Three Rose Corsage

YOU WILL NEED:

3 open pink roses, each 2 1/4" wide
8 sprigs of white silk baby's breath
1 stem silk fern with 5 pieces (fronds)
6 clusters of purple silk heather, each
    cluster 3/4" wide
5 pearl sprays, each spray has 3 pearl
    strands
1 1/4 yards of 1/16" wide white and
    silver ribbon
1 1/4 yards of 1/8" wide pink ribbon
18" length of 22 gauge wire
26 gauge wire
green floral tape
matte acrylic spray

1

2

1   Cut apart the fern pieces (fronds) from
    the main stem. Cut each piece so it is 3
    1/2" long. To make a stem: cut a 6"
    piece of 26 gauge wire and bend it in
    half. Slip the bend over the end of the
    fern and twist the wire in back. Tape
    over the wires.

2   Cut the roses from the main stem. If the
    rose stem is sturdy, tape the stem. If
    not, add a 2" piece of 26 gauge wire
    (see page 1).

3

4

3   Leaving a 1" stem, cut clusters of
    baby's breath and heather from the
    main stem. Tape each piece to a 3"
    piece of 26 gauge wire. Also tape the
    pearl sprays on 3" long wire pieces.

4   Cut three 5" lengths of each ribbon.
    Place a piece of each ribbon together
    and fold in half. Wrap the ends with a 6"
    piece of 26 gauge wire allowing 2" of
    the wire for a stem. Tape. Repeat,
    making two more loops. Set aside.

5

6

7

8

9

11

10

12

5   To make a bow: place both ribbons together and handle as one. Measure 2" from one end and make six loops, each 2" long. Fold a 6" length of 26 gauge wire over the center of the bow and twist the ends to secure the ribbons. Set the bow aside.

6   The corsage is made on a 9" length of 22 gauge wire. As the various items are floral taped to the wire, begin 1/2" to 3/4" below the bottom of each previous item. This will allow part of the flower stem to show and will give room to bend the items as desired. With the heather allow 1" to 1 1/2" of the stem to show. To begin: tape a pearl spray and baby's breath cluster to the end of the wire.

7   Measure 1/2" down the wire and tape a cluster of heather to the left. Add a ribbon tuft to the right and a rose in the center. Attach a cluster of baby's breath and a piece of heather to each side of the rose. A fern goes behind the flowers and the tip of the fern is 2" above the top edge of the rose.

8   Repeat steps 6 and 7 taping a pearl spray, baby's breath, heather, ribbon tuft, rose, two baby's breath clusters (but no heather) and a fern to the wire.

9   Attach the bow diagonally across the corsage. Tape a fern to the left and a pearl spray to the right.

10 Add a cluster of baby's breath, heather (to the right), a pearl spray and a rose. Then a ribbon tuft and fern to the left (these two will be bent down and forward to form the bottom line of the corsage).

11 The last fern, baby's breath, heather and pearl spray are attached to the wire--these last items are bent toward you after the corsage is finished.

12 Trim the stem to 1" long. Tape well to cover all exposed wires. Curve the corsage and spray with matte acrylic spray. The corsage is worn on the left shoulder.

Shoe Clips

FOR BOTH CLIPS YOU WILL NEED:

4 pink roses, each 1" wide and 2 buds
4 clusters of purple silk heather
4 pearl sprays, each spray has 3
strands of pearls
10 leaves, each 1" long
1 1/4 yards of 1/16" wide white & silver
ribbon
1 1/4 yards of 1/8" wide colonial rose
ribbon
26 gauge wire
white floral tape
matte acrylic spray

1

2

TO MAKE EACH CLIP:

1 Floral tape each rose to a 5" piece of 26 gauge wire. Use four roses even though the photo shows three.

2 Place the two ribbons together and handle as one. Measure 1" from an end. Make 6 loops, each 1 1/2" long. Slip a 5" piece of 26 gauge wire in the center of the bow and twist the ends to secure the ribbons.

3 Tape two roses, one bud, one bow, two pearl sprays, and two heather clusters together as shown. Place three leaves above the taped items and two leaves below, tape everything together. Bend the bottom leaves over the stem.

4 Cut the stem to 4 1/2" long. Loop the taped wires as shown, forming a teardrop shape. Then tape the wires together about 1/2" below the bottom leaves. Spray with matte acrylic spray. Bend the loop behind the flowers and pinch together onto the shoe.

3

4

Heart Bridal Train Holder

YOU WILL NEED:

3 yards of 3 3/4" wide white lace ribbon
1 1/2 yards each of 1/8" wide orchid, grape and colonial rose ribbons
6 pink roses, (each 1" wide) and 3 buds
4 rose tri-leaves
6 pieces of 18 gauge wire, each 18" long
26 gauge wire
white floral tape
sewing needle and white thread
glue gun
matte acrylic spray

This unique piece is striking when used for the bride's first dance with her new husband or with her father. The lace heart is hung over the bride's left wrist and her train is draped through the point of the heart. Her wrist then rests on the shoulder of her dancing partner. It looks GREAT in pictures!

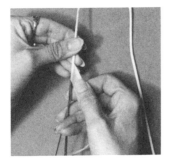

1

2

1. Lay three pieces of the 18 gauge wire side by side. Tape together. Repeat with the other three pieces. Then make one long wire by overlapping the ends of each group by 3". Tape together.

2. Fold the lace ribbon lengthwise around the wire. With needle and thread, sew about 1/2" from the fold, forming a casing around the wire. Gather the lace onto the taped wire.

3

4

3. Circle the wire around overlapping the ends by 3". Tape together. Evenly space the lace around the wire.

4. Bend the wire into a heart shape.

FOR A BOW:

5

6

5   Place the three ribbons together and handle as one. Measure 12" from one end and make a 1 3/4" long loop on each side of your hand.

6   Then make another loop (a cover loop) in the center by bringing the ribbon toward you--up, over and around the thumb.

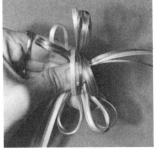

7

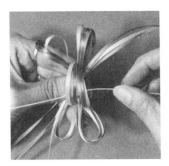

8

7   Repeat steps 5 and 6 making four more loops and another cover loop.

8   Insert a 6" piece of 26 gauge wire into the center of the loops and twist the wire ends to hold the bow securely.

9

10

9   Glue the bow to the left side of the heart, 8" from the center point (measuring along the curve of the heart). Loosely twirl the streamers along the shape of the heart as shown. Glue in a couple of spots to keep the swirled effect.

10 Cut the rose and leaf stems to 1/4" long. Glue 2 tri-leaves around the bow as shown. Glue four roses and a bud into the loops of the bow.

11

12

11 Glue a tri-leaf, a single leaf and a rose among the twirls of ribbon above the bow. Repeat below the bow.

12 Glue another tri-leaf and a rose bud near the ends of the twirled ribbon. For a fuller look, separate the outer edges of the lace. Spray with matte acrylic spray.

Over the Shoulder Corsage

YOU WILL NEED:

2 open white roses, each 2 1/4" wide
1 white rose bud, 1 1/2" long
12 pink roses, (each 1" wide) plus 6 buds
21 rose tri-leaves, each 1/2" to 1" long (may use leaves from other roses)
8 sprigs of dk. pink silk baby's breath
4 pearl sprays, each spray with 3 strands of pearls
1 1/2 yards of 1/16" wide white and silver ribbon
1 1/2 yards of 1/8" wide shocking pink ribbon
26 gauge wire
green floral tape
matte acrylic spray

1

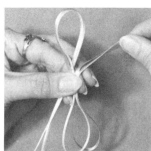

2

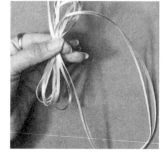

3

4

1   Cut the roses, buds and greens from the main stems leaving as much stem as possible. So that each item in the corsage can be bent to give fullness and dimension to the corsage, it is necessary to floral tape each cut flower, sprig or leaf to a 3" length of wire, see page 1. Set aside.

2   Place both ribbons together and handle as one. Measure 2" from one end and make a 2" long loop. Make another 2" long loop on the other side of your hand.

3   Make two more 2" long loops on each side of your hand. Then make a 6" long loop beneath the bow. Secure with a 6" long piece of wire. Set aside.

4   The total length of the corsage is about 12". Smaller leaves and buds will be used on the ends of the corsage with larger leaves and flowers to fill in the middle. To begin: floral tape together a pearl spray, one tri-leaf, a pink bud, a baby's breath sprig, a pink rose and another pink bud. Be sure to leave 3/4" to 1" of each stem exposed before taping the items together.

5

6

5. Measure 1/2" and add a tri-leaf, pearl spray, pink rose, baby's breath and tri-leaf.

6. Leave 1/2" to 3/4" on each stem before taping items together. Next add a leaf, a pink rose, another leaf and a pink bud. Now add a leaf, baby's breath, pink rose, leaf and pink rose.

7

8

7. Remember to leave space between the items in the corsage. Add a leaf, a pink bud, baby's breath, leaf and pink rose. Then add two larger leaves (if you have them), a white bud and baby's breath.

8. To the right place a pink rose and a leaf. On the left add a pink bud. In the center attach a white rose, 2 leaves, baby's breath, a pink bud and a pink rose.

9

10

9. Add a white rose, 3 leaves, 2 pink roses and the bow made in steps 2 and 3. Let the long loops hang to the outside of the corsage as you continue.

10. The items will be placed closer together now as the corsage tapers to the end. Tape on a sprig of baby's breath, a leaf, a pearl spray and a pink rose.

11

12

11. Now attach 2 leaves, a pink rose, a pearl spray, a pink bud, another leaf and a baby's breath sprig. Trim the stems to 1" long and floral tape the ends well covering all exposed wires. Bend the last items forward to cover the end.

12. Shape the corsage in a slight "S" curve. Spray with matte acrylic spray. The corsage should be worn over the left shoulder with the starting point over the back of the shoulder. Pin on the corsage at two places to hold it securely.

23

Pew Decoration

FOR EACH DECORATION YOU WILL NEED:

2 3/4 yards of 1 1/2" wide white lace ribbon

2 3/4 yards of 1 1/2" wide pink floral satin ribbon (it has satin on one side)

one 18" piece of 22 gauge wire--cloth covered or taped with white floral tape

1 stem ivy about 18" long

10 sprigs of white lily of the valley

green floral tape

matte acrylic spray

Check with the church wedding coordinator before attaching decorations to the pews. They may be hung over the pews, secured with masking tape or attached with a product called Pozy Stik® which is especially made for this purpose.

1   Place the lace ribbon over the satin ribbon and handle as one. Measure 18" from the end. Following the directions on page 21, steps 5 to 8, make a bow with six 4" long loops and one cover loop. Insert the 22 gauge wire into the center of the bow and twist the ends to secure. Set aside.

2   Wrap green floral tape below the last blossom of a lily of the valley sprig. Continue twirling the tape 2" beyond the end of the stem. Attach this sprig to another lily of the valley sprig, then to another and another until the total length is 15". Repeat making two more sprays each 12" long and having 3 sprigs.

3   Place the longer lily of the valley spray in the center of the ivy so the lily tip is 2" below the bottom ivy leaf. A shorter spray is on each side of the ivy. Tape the stems together.

4   Secure the bow to the ivy with the bow wire, trim excess wire. Bend the ivy stem to form a hanger. Spray with matte acrylic spray.

1

2

3

4

Mother's Presentation Bouquet

YOU WILL NEED:

1 large pink rose, 2 1/2" long
1 stem of white silk baby's breath
2 silk fern stems
2 1/4 yards of 5/8" wide pink beaded
   lace ribbon
18" of 18 gauge wire
cloth covered wire
green floral tape
matte acrylic spray

It is a thoughtful gesture when, during the ceremony, flowers are given to each mother-in-law by the new bride and groom.

1

2

3

4

1 Cut the rose and fern stems to 15" long. Floral tape along each stem.

2 Cut the baby's breath into four sections. Floral tape the exposed stems.

3 Place the fern stems so one is just below the other. Position the top of the longest baby's breath stem below the top of the fern. Lay a rose on top of the baby's breath 3" below the tip of the fern. Place a sprig of baby's breath on each side of the rose and one sprig below the base of the rose. Tape all stems together for 2".

4 Measure 12" from the end of the ribbon. Follow the directions on page 21, steps 5-8, to make a bow with eight loops, each 2 1/2" long, and two cover loops. Insert the cloth covered wire into the center of the bow and twist the ends. Tape a 9" piece of 18 gauge wire to the bow wire. Position the bow just above the taped flower stems and tape in place. Spray with matte acrylic spray.

Goblet, Cake Knife or Candleholder Spray

3 pink roses, each 1" wide plus 2 buds
5 clusters of purple silk heather
6 silk ivy leaves, each 1 1/4" long
5 pearl sprays (each with 3 strands of pearls)
2 sprigs of white silk baby's breath
1 1/4 yards of 1/16" wide white & silver ribbon
1 1/4 yards of 1/8" wide colonial rose ribbon
white cloth covered wire
26 gauge wire
green floral tape
white floral tape
matte acrylic spray

1   Cut the flowers and each ivy leaf from the main stem. If the rose stems are sturdy, wrap with green floral tape. If not, add a 2" piece of 26 gauge wire and floral tape. To each cluster of heather, sprig of baby's breath and each ivy leaf, add a 2" piece of 26 gauge wire and wrap with green floral tape.

2   Place both ribbons together and handle as one. Measure 2" from one end and make a bow with 8 loops (each 1 1/2" long) and 2 cover loops, see page 21, steps 5-8. Secure with cloth covered wire.

3   Each item will be floral taped leaving about 1/2" between items. Tape a pearl spray and a heather cluster to an ivy leaf. The pearls extend 1" and the heather 1/2" above the ivy. Center the rosebud on the ivy, tape. Add a sprig of heather and a rose on each side as pictured. A sprig of baby's breath is in the center. Floral tape everything together.

4   Add a pearl spray to the lower left and center. Place ivy leaves to the right and left. Cut stem to 1" long and tape. Tape the remaining materials together, following steps 3 and 4. Tape the two sprays together. Place the bow in the center and twist the wires in back (use these wires to attach the spray and secure with white floral tape). Give a coat of matte acrylic spray.

1

2

3

4

Garter

YOU WILL NEED:

1 white garter
2/3 yard of 3/16" wide white feather
    edge (picot) ribbon
2 sprigs of white lily of the valley
1 cluster of purple silk heather
green floral tape
needle and white sewing thread
cloth covered wire

1

2

1 When sewing flowers to an elastic garter, pull the garter after each stitch to allow the thread to pull slightly. Sew two lily of the valley sprigs to the front of the garter. Overlap the ends of the stems, leaving a 1" gap in the center.

2 Divide the heather cluster in half and wrap the ends of each half with green floral tape.

3

4

3 Sew the heather clusters on top of the lily of the valley.

4 Measure 2" from one end of the ribbon and make 6 loops (each 1" long) and 2 cover loops--see page 21, steps 5-8. Fold a 6" piece of cloth covered wire in half and place in the center of the bow. Twist the ends to secure the ribbon. Cut off excess wire and sew the bow in the center of the flowers.

Framed Wedding Invitation

YOU WILL NEED:

wedding invitation
14" square of both a lace fabric &
* a solid fabric*
1 1/3 yds. of gathered 1 3/4" wide lace
2 1/4 yds. of 3/8" wide rosy mauve
* feather edge (picot) ribbon*
3 yds. of 3/16" wide rosy mauve
* feather edge (picot) ribbon*
2 1/4 yds. of 1/16" wide white and
* silver ribbon*
1 yd. of 1/2" wide scalloped edge lace
8" X 10" Bruna Hoop-Frame™
2 Sweet Suspensions™ bell frames
1 lt. pink and 1 dk. pink rose, 1" wide
3 lt. pink and 2 dk. pink rose buds,
* 1/2" wide*
5 clusters of purple heather
18 rose leaves, 1" long
2 pictures for bell frames
Aleene's Tacky Glue & glue gun
26 gauge wire
matte acrylic spray

1

2

3

4

1   Center the lace and solid fabric pieces over the inner frame; place outer frame on top and press together. Pry the frames apart about 1/8"-1/4" and trim the excess fabric. Press closed. Glue gathered lace to back of frame and the 3/8" ribbon around outer and inner edges of the frame. Glue the invitation to the center of the lace. Glue the 1/2" lace to the edges of the invitation, trim each corner at an angle.

2   Glue the pictures in the bell frames. When dry, glue the 3/16" ribbon to the outer edges of the frames. Use the glue gun to attach the bell frames together and to the frame.

3   For the bow: Place the white and silver ribbon and the 3/16" ribbon together and handle as one. Follow the directions on page 21, steps 5-8, to make a bow with ten loops (each 1 1/2" long) and two cover loops. Glue the rest of the white and silver ribbon on top of the 3/16" ribbon. Twirl the ribbons and spot glue to the frame. Glue the bow to the frame.

4   Use the glue gun to attach leaves into the bow and near the gathered lace. Glue roses, a bud and 3 heather clusters into the bow and the other flowers as shown in the larger photo.